WORSHIP
at HOME

ADVENT *and* CHRISTMAS 2020

Other Resources for Worship and Preaching

The Abingdon Worship Annual
Mary Scifres and B. J. Beu

The Abingdon Preaching Annual

Prepare! An Ecumenical Music and Worship Planner
Mary Scifres and David Bone

The United Methodist Music and Worship Planner
Mary Scifres and David Bone

Find a rich collection of free and subscription resources for weekly worship and preaching at ministrymatters.com/worship.

ADVENT *and* CHRISTMAS 2020

WORSHIP
at HOME

MARY SCIFRES
AND B. J. BEU

Abingdon Press™
Nashville, TN

WORSHIP AT HOME: ADVENT AND CHRISTMAS 2020
Copyright © 2020 by Mary Scifres and B. J. Beu

ISBN: 9781791020279

20 21 22 23 24 25 26 27 28 29—10 9 8 7 6 5 4 3 2 1
MANUFACTURED IN THE UNITED STATES OF AMERICA

CONTENTS

INTRODUCTION

Introducing a New Series

Whether you are worshiping from home or leading others in worship this holiday season, we've written this book to support and nourish your worship life and spiritual formation. The first in a series of home-based worship books that follow the church year, the Worship at Home series will enhance your worship life, whether you are worshiping live, virtually, or in a hybrid form of both. To explore how you might use this resource as an individual, a family, a pastor, or a congregation, read the following section entitled **How to Use This Resource**. As this is the first volume of this resource, we welcome your feedback and hope that you will email your ideas to us. To help the series support you, your ministry, and your worship life, you'll find our contact information, along with a free offer, at the end of this introduction.

The Gift of Holiday Worship at Home

Growing up, I loved the idyllic world of the television series *Little House on the Prairie*. Each episode's problems were resolved in an hour, and the family seemed holistic, healthy, and happy. I particularly loved scenes when Laura and Mary would sit at their Pa's knee to listen to him read scripture or play the fiddle as Ma peacefully knitted or cuddled with their baby sister Carrie. I later discovered that the books captured a very different picture of pioneer settlers in the Midwest and great plains states of the 18th century. The life of Laura Ingalls Wilder, as recounted in her children's novels, was far from idyllic. I was fascinated by Laura's objections to Sundays and the quiet, stoic worship required of them. I was struck with how different Sundays would have been if the settlers had followed the television script rather than the somber tradition of their day. Surely, worship at home could be idyllic. Families could gather and enjoy reading scripture, sharing music, and enjoying the gift of time together. This vision never left me and has guided me over the years.

As a young child, I was blessed by big sisters who played piano and loved the holidays. We would laugh and celebrate, while singing carols around the piano. I'd even invite our parents' friends to join us when they would gather at our house for holiday parties. My mom, who to this day insists she cannot carry a tune, even joined in the fun, singing with gusto as we celebrated the season with music. After my sisters moved away, and I remained the only child at home, my parents would sit quietly, sipping coffee or wine, and listen to me practice a solo for Christmas Eve or simply play through my favorite carols. They would hum quietly as I sang boldy. Other times, my mom would put on my favorite holiday albums, while we talked about which carols were our favorites and why they meant so much to us. More than any other season, the holidays always provided fond memories of worship and praise—memories acquired in our home with family and friends.

As a young pastor, my youth coordinator not only created a home Advent tradition for her preschool son and toddler daughter, she invited our entire church family to follow suit. Every November, we would gather as a congregation for an evening of carol singing and crafts. Each family would create their own Advent wreath to take home, complete with a devotional guide from Abingdon Press and Cokesbury. Thus began my personal home worship tradition for the holidays—a tradition began before I even had a spouse or a child. Each morning, I would light the candle, read the day's devotional (or the week's devotion daily), follow the Advent calendar, and focus my thoughts on the season that had always been so precious to me.

When B. J. and I had a child of our own, our son developed a fascination with Nativity scenes and Advent candles. Our Advent tradition expanded to include the purchase of a Nativity set, and the creation of a new Advent wreath or Advent calendar for him each year. Church members joined in the fun and his collection grew. In those youngest years, he loved setting up and playing with his various Nativity sets, but none more than the cloth one that posed no worries of Mom rushing over to avoid a broken character. He loved lighting the candles or following the Advent calendar, as we counted down the days to Christmas. But eventually, he grew weary of the tradition, finding it more arduous than enjoyable, reminding me of the young Laura Ingalls and her frustration with Sunday traditions. So we let some traditions go and created new rituals we could all enjoy: Christmas caroling, making Christmas cookies, driving in festive neighborhoods to revel at their beautiful light displays, and visiting Hallmark and other local gift stores for their annual holiday open houses. In their own ways, even these rituals became a sort of "home worship" for our family.

Celebrating Christmas in big sanctuaries, cathedrals, or even concert halls with choirs and orchestras is a modern phenomenon. So is worship as we know it today. In the fourth century, Christians began building structures to hold worship. Even so, worship continued in homes and neighborhood buildings, with only occasional pilgrimages to cathedrals and basilicas. It remains so in countries where Christianity is illegal, suppressed, or simply rare. Increasingly, new church starts pick up this ancient and intimate form of worship. Households gather for study and prayer, friends break bread together, and small groups become the centerpiece for new faith communities. This slow-growing movement has taken hold at different paces and in different formats since the 1970s.

In the midst of a global pandemic, most church-going Christians will be celebrating Christmas in new and different ways—some with gladness, some with sorrow. Whether you find yourself yearning for days gone by or excitedly looking forward to a quieter, simpler season, this book is our gift to you. In these pages you will find resources to create and claim new traditions and rituals for yourself and your loved ones, regardless of the year's circumstances. Even if you have the opportunity to gather for live worship with a faith community, you will find here words, songs, activities, and rituals for mapping your own spiritual journey through Advent and Christmas. Use these services with family and friends, or as an opportunity for personal devotion. You may even use these resources to enhance live and large-group gatherings of which you are a part.

If you pick this book up in a year when you are overwhelmed and distracted by holiday parties and church events, you will find here an invitation to return to the quieter gift of this season. Read the words and prayers silently or aloud, sing or listen to the suggested songs, reflect on the poetry of the song lyrics and the wisdom of the scriptures and stories, and participate in the activities and rituals that help you focus on the meaning of Christ's arrival and presence in your life. Share this book with a spouse, a child, a life partner, a friend, your family, a small group, or even neighborhood friends. (Share these services via video conference if needs be.) Immanuel, "God with us," will be with you, perhaps more so than ever, for the need is great.

Whatever your situation and the state of the world, we hope you will find inspiration and ideas in these pages to strengthen your spirit and to sustain your soul.

Yours on the Journey,
Mary Scifres & B. J. Beu

Contact us at admin@maryscifres.com or learn more about our work at www.maryscifres.com.

SPECIAL OFFER: FREE RESOURCE
Enjoy a free ebook *The Art of Extravagant Welcome: Sharing God's Love* by visiting https://maryscifres.simplero.com/adventbook.

HOW TO USE THIS BOOK

Getting Ready

If your worship life is centered at home this year, or if you simply want to add home-based worship to supplement your church's worship life, this book is for you. We invite you to read each worship service beforehand and decide how to best use the resources they contain. Choose the activities, words, and songs that fit your preferences and your traditions. When you are ready to worship, you can do so in several ways. First, you can follow the order of service as written, having previously chosen your song and response options. Alternately, you can select a few worship elements to create a brief time of devotion. Another option is to spread out any or all of the worship elements during the week. Many people choose to repeat a meaningful part of the service, like lighting the Advent candles, every day of the week, not just on Sunday. The more you prepare for worship during the Advent and Christmas seasons, the more meaningful worship will be. See our list of recommended **Things to Gather before Advent Begins** at the end of this chapter.

This edition of *Worship at Home* focuses worship on the Advent themes of peace, hope, joy, and love—themes represented by the Advent candles lit each week. Following ancient tradition, we invite you to light Advent candles (and the Christ candle once Christmas Eve arrives) throughout Advent and the Christmas season, which ends on Epiphany. To prepare, you may purchase or create a Christmas Advent candle set beforehand, with or without a wreath. Such sets have five candles: a white Christ candle surrounded by four tapers. (Although the Christ candle is usually larger in diameter than your Advent tapers, your candles can be of any size or shape.) Traditionally, all four Advent candles are purple, the liturgical color of royalty, or three are purple and one is pink or rose, the liturgical color of joy. The latter follows traditions that celebrate the Third Sunday of Advent (also known as Gaudete Sunday) with a pink-colored candle. Many craft sites and craft stores have instructions to help you create your own Advent wreath and set of candles. For safety and ease of use, feel free to use battery-powered candles, particularly when worshiping alone or with young children.

Beginning on Christmas Eve, we will invite you to reflect on characters in the nativity scene at Christ's birth. Having a crèche (nativity set) in your worship space will enhance your worship experience and give young children a tangible image to understand the season. If you don't have a crèche, bookmark an online image using a search engine like Google Images, or print an image to have available for worship. (Fair warning: Good nativity images are surprisingly difficult to find online.)

Similarly, some of the services' Sending Activities suggest a craft or providing a gift to neighbors or strangers. Reading through the activities before Advent will give you time to order craft supplies or gifts beforehand. Some activities include the use of: Advent calendars, tea lights or votive candles, index or greeting cards, peace and love ornaments, Christmas cookies, and small gifts or plants to surprise people with during the season. You don't need to purchase a thing to worship at home this holiday season, but if an idea captures your fancy, we wanted to give you time to prepare.

Ideas for Individuals and Families

Home-based worship allows you to tailor certain worship elements to fit your preferences. Make decisions to create what will be most meaningful for you and those worshiping with you. Do you enjoy singing Christmas carols, or do you prefer to silently allow the music to wash over you? Do you prefer instrumental or vocal arrangements? Do you like to discuss scripture or do you prefer to reflect quietly; or do you like scripture to inspire you to action? Below, we list the **Worship Elements** where choices are offered each week.

Using This Resource in Congregational Worship

Although written with individuals, families, and home-based worship in mind, this book also provides excellent resources for pastors and churches yearning for new ways of creating worship together. This resource can help congregations stay connected, even while worshiping from home. It can also help pastors and church leaders provide a structured worship order just as written here, or easily adaptable for use in a variety of settings during the Advent and Christmas seasons. Many church leaders will use this book as their Sunday morning worship plan. Others may use it to add a weekly or daily vespers service throughout the season. Some may find the children's candle lighting litanies ideal for a short Sunday School lesson via prerecorded or live video conference calls. Others may lift a few segments for use in youth group gatherings or in other small group worship experiences and discussions. We invite you to use this resource in whatever way best serves you and your congregation.

When leading a congregation or group with this worship resource, you can advise people to collect the appropriate Advent candles and other supplies they will need beforehand. Or you may choose to purchase the supplies, as your budget allows, and deliver them to those who will be worshiping from home. Deliveries may be made through a shipping provider like Cokesbury, through a mailing from the church office, or by personal delivery when safe to do so. While some churches have delivered hymnals to church members worshiping at home, we've eliminated this need by choosing hymns that are readily available online—many of which may be printed by right of public domain. See the complete list of Recommended Hymns and Songs at the end of this article in case you want to print up a songbook with lyrics for your group of people.

Worship Elements

Lighting the Candles includes two options. The first provides extended meditation and centering time, which may be better suited for adults than young children. The second follows the Seder tradition of having children ask questions. Its responsive format provides an explanation for the meaning of each Advent and the Christ candle and why we light them. Parents and adults who choose to use the option for children may want to extend the question and answers into a lengthier conversation or perhaps come back to adult meditation at a later time in the week. Adults who choose the meditative option may want to view the responsive option to better understand the meaning of the candles.

Poems presented as spoken word are a beautiful part of each Advent service, as are recommended YouTube music videos. You can access those with a smartphone, tablet, computer, or smart TV with the YouTube app. Again, planning ahead can help. Find the video link and bookmark it before beginning worship so you don't have to interrupt the flow to find a video.

Song selections have multiple options. If you have a hymnal or songbook of carols, you can open to the song and sing along. At the end of this article, you'll find the complete list of songs we've recommended, along with hymn numbers from several popular hymnals. You can also consult the index or table of contents of your favorite hymnal and find most songs listed alphabetically by the song's title or first line. If you like to sing but don't have a hymnal, we've also referenced YouTube options, some that include lyrics. If you don't care to sing, you can simply enjoy the music in the videos, often set to stunning background imagery.

Scripture Readings may either be read by one person or divided up into parts for multiple readers. On the Third Sunday of Advent, Mary's Magnificat (Luke 1:46b-55) is written responsively and works well when read as such, but may also be read by one person.

Responses to the Word during the four Sundays of Advent have two options. The first is a physical activity to reinforce the **Meditation** on the day's scriptures. The second is a set of questions to help you enter more deeply into the message and meaning of the day. You can choose one or both, just as you can choose one, two, or all of the questions for thought or discussion.

Finally, there are a multitude of **Sending Activities** to help you put your faith into action throughout the week. You may choose to focus on one, or several each week. You may choose to mix it up from week to week. Some of you may want to see how many activities you can do throughout the week to keep the meaning of the season before you each day. This is a resource for *you*. Use it in the way that best strengthens your experience of this holiday season.

Creating a Worship Space in Your Home

Creating a sacred space in which to worship requires intentionality, planning, and effort. Ideally, this is a space that can remain set up throughout the Advent and Christmas seasons. If you already have a centering or meditation space, use that. If not, pay attention to your body. Find a place that feels open and comfortable. If the space makes your body feel cramped or closed off, your spirit will have a difficult time opening up to the holy. Whether we are physical beings having spiritual experiences, or we are spiritual being having physical experiences, the result is the same—our body, minds, and spirits are intertwined and influence each other. Once you find a space that feels right, you may want to set up an altar on a small table. Swathe the altar with a fabric covering. We use a prayer shawl that was knitted for B. J. when he was undergoing cancer treatment. Decorate your altar with a cross or other sacred objects. These objects can be literally anything that help you feel grounded in God's love and acceptance, or that connect you to a sense of the holy. Leave enough space on the altar for an Advent wreath, complete with candles. If you have a crèche or nativity set, place it somewhere easily visible while you worship. As each of these worship services recommend YouTube videos, be sure you have a smartphone, tablet, computer, or smart TV with the YouTube app in the room with easy access to the internet. Once you are finished, dedicate the space to God. Thank God for meeting you in this place and for being with you during your Advent and Christmas journey.

Things to Gather before Advent Begins

Before Advent begins, you may find it helpful to gather some or all of these items to enhance your worship experiences. Gather what you want and need, and leave the rest!

- a dedicated worship space with smart phone, tablet, computer, or smart TV with the YouTube app; and easy internet access
- piano and hymnal if you prefer to play and sing
- an altar with Christmas Advent Candle Set with matches, lighter, or batteries (if electronic)
- crèche (nativity set)
- print copies of the day's worship service, or access the electronic version on your tablet, phone, or computer
- a journal or notepad if you like to write reflections down
- craft or gift supplies for selected Sending Activities

Recommended Hymns and Songs

Most of our recommended hymns and carols can be found in any Christmas songbook or hymnal for those who want to play and sing during these worship experiences. To find a hymn in your favorite hymnal or songbook, turn to the alphabetical index at the end of the hymnal. Most hymns are easily referenced from that list. Occasionally, there may be an alphabetized table of contents near the beginning, but that is more likely in a songbook than in a hymnal. Online at www.hymnary.org, you can also find lyrics for all of these hymns. Throughout these worship services, we also recommend videos that provide accompaniment, lyrics, and meaningful performances of these sacred songs, so you can listen and sing even without a hymnal or songbook.

We are including a list of hymns and hymn numbers from the United Methodist, Presbyterian, Episcopal, and Lutheran churches. Unless otherwise indicated (* or +), the United Methodist lyrics may be reprinted by right of public domain. Indicated items have limitations noted below.

SONG TITLE	UMC	PCUSA	TEC	ELCA
O Little Town of Bethlehem	230	121	79	279
It Came Upon the Midnight Clear	218	123	89	282
Come, Thou Long-Expected Jesus	196	82	66	254
Hail to the Lord's Anointed	203	149	616	311
O Come, O Come, Emmanuel*	211	88	56	257
Joy to the World	246	134	100	267
Lo, How a Rose E'er Blooming+	216	129	81	272
Love Came Down at Christmas	242		84	
Angels We Have Heard on High	238	113	96	289
What Child Is This	219	145	115	296
Hark! the Herald Angels Sing	240	119	87	270
Angels from the Realms of Glory	220	143	93	275
Silent Night	239	122	111	281
This Little Light of Mine	585			
The First Noel	245	147	109	300
We Three Kings	254	151	128	

*The PCUSA version of "O Come, O Come, Emmanuel" may be reprinted by right of public domain, whereas the UM version is copyright-protected.
+Verses 1 and 2 of "Lo, How a Rose E'er Blooming" may be reprinted by right of public domain. Verse 3 is copyright-protected.

UMC: *The United Methodist Hymnal.* Nashville: The United Methodist Publishing House, 1989.

PCUSA: *Glory to God: The Presbyterian Hymnal.* Louisville: Presbyterian Publishing, 2013.

TEC: *The Hymnal 1982.* New York: The Church Hymnal Corporation, 1985.

ELCA: *Evangelical Lutheran Worship.* Minneapolis: Augsburg Fortress, 2006.

CHAPTER 1
FIRST SUNDAY
OF ADVENT: PEACE

Gathering Music:
"Bless the Broken Road"

The Piano Guys *(piano)*
https://youtu.be/2ZQK5NmVG1g

Centering Words

"In the beginning was a home—and the home was God's peace, and God was peace."

~ Lo The Poet

(Refer to the previous chapter, "How to Use This Resource," on setting up a Christmas Advent Candle set.)

Lighting the Advent Candle of Peace
(with adults)

(If you are worshiping alone or with a group of adults, light a purple candle and follow these instructions.)

As you gaze upon the flickering candle, reflect on an aspect of God's peace that seems missing from your life—something that would make God's peace your true home. Once this is clear in your mind, center your attention on your breath. Breathe this peace deeply into your lungs and hold your breath for a moment, feeling God's peace spread throughout your body, becoming your home. As you exhale, focus on casting out the worries, fears and insecurities that hinder the peace you seek—the peace that the Spirit offers us each and every moment of our lives. Continue to breathe in and out until you feel rooted in Christ's peace.

–OR–

Lighting the Advent Candle of Peace (with children)

(If you are worshiping with children, help the youngest child light the first purple candle. Explain that you will light an additional candle each week until the white candle is lit to celebrate Christ's birth on Christmas Eve. Gaze on the candles quietly before reading the response below; or use the response to begin a conversation on how the children see the candles. With older children, try reflecting the questions back to them, inviting them to provide their own answers.)

Child	Why do we light Advent candles?
Adult	*Advent candles remind us of the light of God coming into the world at Christmas.*
Child	Why do we only light one candle today?
Adult	*We only light one candle because this is the first week of Advent.*
Child	Why do we light this candle?
Adult	*This is the Advent candle of Peace. We light it because God is our source of peace, and because Jesus is the Prince of Peace.*
Child	So that's why we light the Advent candles.
Adult	*That's why we light the Advent candles.*

Poetic Reflection

"For Unto Us—PEACE," Lo The Poet
https://youtu.be/y3KxUDKUEQU

Opening Prayer

Your home is peace, Author of Shalom,
> for you are Peace—
>> peace that is a resting place,
>>> when I feel lost and forsaken;
>> peace that brings comfort and mercy,
>>> when I am weary and heavy laden;
>> peace that cradles me in abundant love,
>>> when I find myself outside in the cold;
>> peace that flows in a spring of living water
>>> when I am in the wilderness of life.

Open my heart, Prince of Peace,
> that I may receive you into my life this day.

I am ready for your coming,
> the coming of Peace. Amen.

Scripture of Praise (Isaiah 52:7)

How beautiful upon the mountains
> are the feet of a messenger
> who proclaims peace,
> who brings good news,
> who proclaims salvation,
> who says to Zion, "Your God rules!"

Song: "O Little Town of Bethlehem"

(Piano with lyrics)
https://youtu.be/fH3ppMy8xzY
Gaither Vocal Band *(a cappela vocals)*
https://youtu.be/CwfkGj51S2c
Sarah McLachlan *(vocals)*
https://youtu.be/W3mq6s1zQWo

Scripture Reading
(Micah 5:2, 4-5a, adapted)

As for you, Bethlehem of Ephrathah,
 though you are the least significant clan of Judah,
 out of you will come one
 who is to be a ruler in Israel on my behalf.
His origin is from remote times, from ancient days.
He will stand and shepherd his flock
 in the strength of the Lord,
 in the majesty of the name of the Lord his God.
They will dwell secure,
 because he will surely become great throughout the earth.
And he will be our peace.

Meditation

From Bethlehem, the least significant clan of Judah, comes one who is greatest—one who will rule and shepherd God's people with righteousness and peace. Bethlehem literally means "house of bread," which is fitting, since Christ is not just our Shepherd, Christ is the very bread of life. The strength of the Lord and the majesty of God is not found in tasty falafels or really good Sabbath Challah, but in the living bread that came down from heaven. This ruler gives us food that truly satisfies, for it nurtures the spirit within us. This is a day to celebrate the peace that comes from eating the bread of heaven—a bread often scorned by those who are starving to death from spiritual hunger.

Response to the Word

Hold a piece of bread in cupped hands at the level of your heart. Invite Christ to be present in the bread. Rest in his promise to be with you always when you eat this bread in remembrance of him. Give thanks to God and let your heart fill with gratitude as you place the bread in your mouth and tenderly and lovingly partake of this sacramental gift.

–OR–

4

Response to the Word

Reflect on Lo the Poet's "For Unto Us—PEACE."

• What does it mean that Peace has left its country to make of us citizens of peace?

• What restlessness do you want to be set free from?

• Where do you find comfort in your crazy?

• Where are the shut up places in your hearts? How might this Advent season help you open more fully to God and to others?

• What does it mean that God became an immigrant that we might become natives through Nativity?

• Lo the Poet reminds us that Jesus's tiny hands are "destined to build the kingdom on earth as it is in heaven." Where do you see this in the world today? How are your hands connected with Jesus's hands in creating God's realm?

Song: "It Came Upon the Midnight Clear"

Maranatha *(vocals with lyrics)*
https://youtu.be/XQjpDKKPDK4

Sixpence None *(vocals with lyrics)*
https://youtu.be/Xw3wDU5YAaM

Blessing

Peace has come.
Be open to its promise.
Be prepared to lay your burdens down
    and rest in the Prince of Peace.
Be ready to receive Shalom,
    the coming of Peace.

Sending Activities

(Choose an activity or come up with your own way to share God's peace in the week ahead.)

- Place a tea-light or votive candle on each doorstep in your neighborhood with an index card saying: "Wishing you the light of God's peace."

- Send emails or place calls to friends and families who are struggling to know God's peace.

- Make a donation or give your time to a charity that helps people without homes find shelter and safety; or to a charity that provides food and support for people who are food-insecure.

- Create a simple peace sign ornament for your tree, or invite everyone in the family to create several, sharing the extras with neighbors and friends. A simple method is to print out a peace sign on sturdy paper, trace the design onto white poster board or card stock, cut out the ornament, and decorate with paint, crayons, or glitter.

- Listen to "Do You Hear What I Hear," paying attention to messages of peace and guidance that Christ may be offering you as the holiday season begins. Home Free's version is available here: https://youtu.be/wIQQDYaoWpc.

- If you have an Advent calendar, begin counting down the days to Christmas, usually around December 1.

CHAPTER 2
SECOND SUNDAY OF ADVENT: HOPE

Gathering Music:
"The Mission/How Great Thou Art"

The Piano Guys *(cello and piano)*
https://youtu.be/CHV6BjuQOZQ

Centering Words

"In the beginning was a dream—and the dream was God's hope, and God was hope."

~ Lo The Poet

Lighting the Advent Candle of Hope
(with adults)

(If you are worshiping alone or with a group of adults, relight the Advent candle of Peace, then light a second purple candle and follow these instructions.)

As you gaze upon the flickering candles, reflect on the promise of God's hope in your life—a hope that may only live in your dreams. Centering your attention on your breath, allow this hope to fill you as you breathe deeply, inviting Christ's presence into your life. Hold each breath for a moment, feeling

God's hope spread throughout your body. As you exhale, focus on releasing the personal failures, and the doubts that keep you from claiming the hope to which you were called in Christ. Continue to breathe in and out until you feel rooted in this hope.

–OR–

Lighting the Advent Candle of Hope (with children)

(If you are worshiping with children, help the second youngest child relight Advent candle of Peace before lighting a second purple candle. Explain that you will light an additional candle each week until the white candle is lit to celebrate Christ's birth on Christmas Eve. Gaze on the candles quietly before reading the response below; or use the response to begin a conversation on how the children see the candles. With older children, try reflecting the questions back to them, inviting them to provide their own answers.)

Child	Why do we light Advent candles?
Adult	*Advent candles remind us of the light of God coming into the world at Christmas.*
Child	How many candles do we light today?
Adult	*We light two candles because this is the second week of Advent.*
Child	Why do we relight the first candle?
Adult	*We relight the Advent candle of Peace because this is a season of peace.*
Child	Why do we light the second candle?
Adult	*This is the Advent candle of Hope. We light it because Jesus is the hope of the world.*
Child	So that's why we light the Advent candles.
Adult	*That's why we light the Advent candles.*

Poetic Reflection

"For Unto Us—HOPE," Lo The Poet
https://youtu.be/q9CGoXMzvow

Opening Prayer

Your dream is hope, Holy One, for you are Hope—
    hope that turns a lowly manger
      into a mighty throne;
    hope that turns lowly shepherds
      into the first witnesses of your good news;
    hope that turns selfish ambition
      into dreams of faithful servanthood;
    hope that turns longing for salvation
      into the blessings of eternal life.
Heal my fear and doubt,
    that I may dream your hope
      into my life this day.
I am ready for your coming,
    the coming of Hope. Amen.

Psalm of Praise (Psalm 27:14)

Hope in the LORD!
Be strong! Let your heart take courage!
Hope in the LORD!

Song: "Come, Thou Long-Expected Jesus"

Red Mountain Music *(vocals with lyrics)*
https://youtu.be/vRAFQCOkjgE
Fernando Ortega *(piano with lyrics)*
https://youtu.be/0dmO8UPlWoo

Scripture Reading (Isaiah 11:1, 5-6, 9a)

A shoot will grow up from the stump of Jesse;
    a branch will sprout from his roots.
Righteousness will be the belt around his hips,
    and faithfulness the belt around his waist.
The wolf will live with the lamb,
    and the leopard will lie down with the young goat;
    the calf and the young lion will feed together,
    and a little child will lead them.
They won't harm or destroy anywhere
    on my holy mountain.

Meditation

How big is our hope? Jesse, a simple shepherd in Bethlehem, was King David's father. From his stump a branch is promised—one in David's lineage who will wear righteousness and faithfulness as a belt. But this shoot will also usher in the peaceable kingdom—a proverbial return to the garden of Eden, where none shall hurt or destroy on all God's holy mountain. We all know the joke: "The wolf may lie down with the lamb, but the lamb won't get much sleep." In the world we live in, we'd settle for one who wore righteousness and faithfulness as a belt. We don't expect to go back to the garden. But God invites us to set our sights higher, and to make our hope bigger. How big is our hope? We get what we settle for.

Response to the Word

Look around your home and take note of something that is broken or needs fixing. Pay attention to your feelings, especially if it is something that has bothered you for a while. Put a mental plan in place to get it fixed and give yourself a timeline to do so. Make a promise to yourself to hold to your plan. Find hope in this promise; and trust yourself to see it through. If you can trust yourself in something simple, you will grow to trust God in things that are much more important. Hope blooms where it is planted and tended.

–OR–

Response to the Word

Reflect on Lo the Poet's "For Unto Us—Hope."

- What and where do you sense God's dream invading our sleeping world?

- How might we open our eyes and embrace this dream with God?

- When has hope turned your doubts into dreams?

- Like unnoticed shepherds of old, who might be the most crucial witnesses to the good news of God's presence and promised hope today?

- How might we notice and hear the witness they bear?

(Sing along with the song suggested below or simply listen, allowing the gift of music to bring you hope. If you prefer a traditional hymn, we suggest "Hail to the Lord's Anointed," or whatever favorite seasonal hymn speaks to you. Most hymnals have Advent and Christmas hymns grouped together in one section. Check your table of contents. You'll find Advent hymns in The United Methodist Hymnal #198–216 and Christmas carols #217–251.)

Song: "Hope Is Born Again"

Jim Brickman and Point of Grace *(piano and vocals with lyrics)*
https://youtu.be/AdqW6j1H6Vk

Benediction

Hope has come.
Be open to its many disguises.
Be prepared to accept what you truly need.
Be ready to receive the Promised One,
    the coming of Hope.

Sending Activities

(Choose an activity or come up with your own way to share God's hope in the week ahead.)

- Write the words of Psalm 27:14 from the Psalm of Praise above, or use your own words of hope, to share with friends and neighbors via email, cards, letters, or phone calls.

- Call or email your church or your favorite charity and ask if there is a family, individual, or even a staff member who is in need of hope this season. Offer to provide money, tangible goods, or the gift of time to help bring hope where it's needed most.

- Set up a crèche (Nativity set) or find an image of one online. Let yourself enter into the story of the Nativity in order to find a reason to hope. As you place the characters, or simply look at them, think about (or discuss) the fears and the hopes each character might have experienced at the birth of Jesus. If talking with small children, invite them to give a name of hope to each character: i.e., Mary the Magnificent, Shepherd Daring Darrell, etc.

CHAPTER 3
THIRD SUNDAY OF ADVENT: JOY

Gathering Music:
"O Come, O Come, Emmanuel"

The Piano Guys *(cello and piano)*
https://youtu.be/iO7ySn-Swwc

Centering Words

"In the beginning was a song—and the song was God's joy, and God was joy."

~ Lo The Poet

Lighting the Advent Candle of Joy
(with adults)

(If you are worshiping alone or with a group of adults, relight the Advent candles of Peace and Hope, then light a third purple candle and follow these instructions.)

As you gaze upon the flickering candles, reflect on the song of joy that God is singing in and through your life—even if the words and melody seem too faint to hear. Centering your attention on your breath, allow this song of joy to set your heart singing. Breathe deeply, and with each breath you take, listen for the harmonies your soul longs to add to the song. Hold each breath for a moment, feeling God's joy in every beat of your heart. As you exhale, focus on releasing the things that steal your joy, the things that make you doubt the Singer and the song singing within and through you. Continue to breathe in and out until you cannot keep from singing.

–OR–

Lighting the Advent Candle of Joy (with children)

(If you are worshiping with children, help the third youngest child light the Advent candle of Peace and Hope before lighting a third candle that is either pink or purple. Explain that you will light an additional candle each week until the white candle is lit to celebrate Christ's birth on Christmas Eve. If you use a pink candle, ask, "Why pink?" and encourage the children to come up with their own answers. Traditions vary, so there is no "right" answer, but rose is the liturgical color of joy, whereas purple is the liturgical color of royalty, focusing on the coming King. Gaze on the candles quietly before reading the response below; or use the response to begin a conversation on how the children see the candles. With older children, try reflecting the questions back to them, inviting them to provide their own answers.)

Child	Why do we light Advent candles?
Adult	*Advent candles remind us of the light of God coming into the world at Christmas.*
Child	How many candles do we light today?
Adult	*We light three candles because this is the third week of Advent.*
Child	Why do we relight the first two candles?
Adult	*We relight the Advent candles of Peace and Hope because this is a season of peace and hope.*
Child	Why do we light the third candle?
Adult	*This is the Advent candle of Joy. We light it because Mary sang for joy when she heard she would give birth to Jesus, who is the joy of the world.*
Child	So that's why we light the Advent candles.
Adult	*That's why we light the Advent candles.*

Poetic Reflection

"For Unto Us—JOY," Lo The Poet
https://youtu.be/M_lqgLFUkgY

Opening Prayer

Your song is joy, Singer of Creation, for you are Joy—
    joy that fills the empty with good things;
    joy that sings light into the darkness;
    joy that echoes with angelic song;
    joy that births hope in the midst of despair.
Open my lips to sing your praise
    and receive your melody in my life.
I am ready for your coming,
    the coming of Joy. Amen.

Scripture of Praise
(Philippians 4:4-5 NIV)

Rejoice in the Lord always.
I will say it again: Rejoice!
Let your gentleness be evident to all.
The Lord is near.

Song: "O Come, O Come, Emmanuel"

Megan Smith's channel *(choir with lyrics)*
https://youtu.be/7xtpJ4Q_Q-4

Scripture Reading
(Luke 1:46b-55, NIV adapted)

(This scripture may be read responsively.)

Mary said: "My soul glorifies the Lord
and my spirit rejoices in God my Savior,
   who has been mindful of me,
   a humble servant.
From now on all generations will call me blessed,
   for the Mighty One has done great things for me—
   holy is God's name.
God's mercy extends to those who fear the Lord,
from generation to generation.
   God's arm is strong, performing mighty deeds,
   and scattering the proud in their inmost thoughts.
The mighty one has brought down rulers from their thrones
but has lifted up the humble.
   The Lord has filled the hungry with good things
   but has sent the rich away empty.
God has helped Israel, the Lord's servant,
remembering to be merciful
to Abraham and his descendants forever,
   fulfilling the promises to our ancestors."

Meditation

Mary's Magnificat, or song of praise, mirrors Hannah's song of praise in 1 Samuel 2:1-10. But this is more than beautiful poetry; this conveys the joyful heart of a young girl who has every reason to be anything but joyful. Convincing your friends and family, particularly your fiancé, that you carry a child conceived by the Holy Spirit is a tough sell. Yet Mary's heart is filled with joy, knowing who God is bringing into the world through her. Ninety percent of the spiritual life is about letting go . . . of control, the need to be right, the need to appear spotless and blameless in the eyes of other. As the old saying goes: Let go and let God. Mary is the perfect vessel to carry the Son of God precisely because she is humble, and because she is willing to say with Jesus in the garden: "Not my will but thy will be done." In aligning with, and finding joy in, God's purposes, Mary became the unshakable example of faith that has been venerated by millions of Christians through the ages. Today is a day to realize that joy does not come from getting what we want, but from receiving what God is doing through us—even when it seems like this is anything but a blessing.

Response to the Word

If your health allows, go outside without a coat for a minute or two. When the winter begins to slowly rob you of warmth, step back inside and be joyful that you have a place to live and escape the elements. Pay attention to your body, as goosebumps give way to a luxurious sensation of comfort and security. Look at the place you call home, however humble, and give thanks for your blessings. Then offer a silent prayer for those who are not housed, those who spend their days and nights seeking the shelter you often take for granted.

–OR–

Response to the Word

Reflect on Lo the Poet's "For Unto Us—JOY."

- How do you sense God's joy in Jesus's birth stories and in Jesus's entry into the world?

- Where have you seen signs of God's joy in recent weeks or in this past year?

- When have you felt that sorrow might swallow the story whole?

- Where have you heard joy wrapped in song during Advent?

- Where or how are you discovering truth wrapped in mystery as you seek to embrace Christ's presence during this holiday season?

17

Song: "Joy to the World"

Megan Smith's channel *(choir with lyrics)*
https://youtu.be/kyciMYZq2-Y
Celtic Woman *(vocals)*
https://youtu.be/VDmIddF7DfQ

Benediction

Joy has come,
for the Lord has come.
Be open to its splendor.
Be prepared to sing it in your heart.
Be ready to receive the Singer of Creation,
    the coming of Joy.

Sending Activities

(Choose an activity or come up with your own way to share God's joy in the week ahead.)

- If you have the ability or technology to perform or play music outdoors, surprise your neighbors by inviting them to come and listen to a short holiday concert. Sing or play joy-filled Christmas carols from your driveway or deck, reminding people to sing along only if it is safe to do so. Otherwise, encourage people to hum quietly as you all enjoy the gift of joy that comes through music.

- Deliver a poinsettia, potted plant, or a simple holiday gift anonymously to a neighbor's front porch or a favorite church or charity's front office. Include a card that says, "Joy to the world and joy to you!" or "Thank you for bringing joy to the world!" Alternately, send emails or cards with a message of joy.

- Make Christmas cookies with frosting and sprinkles. As you decorate each cookie, think of one thing that brings you joy, then pray for this source of joy. If you do this activity with children or other family members, take turns talking about the things that bring you joy as you decorate.

CHAPTER 4
FOURTH SUNDAY
OF ADVENT: LOVE

Gathering Music:
"Lo, How a Rose E'er Blooming"

Mannheim Steamroller *(instrumental)*
https://youtu.be/ztN33cWu1VQ

Centering Words

"In the beginning was a light—and the light was God's love; and God was love."
~ Lo The Poet

Lighting the Advent Candle of Love
(with adults)

(If you are worshiping alone or with a group of adults, relight the Advent candles of Peace, Hope, and Joy, then light the fourth purple candle and follow these instructions.)

As you gaze upon the flickering candles, reflect on the light of God's love that shines in and through your life—even in the darkest night when clouds shroud the moon and stars. Centering your attention on your breath, allow this light to fill you and burst forth from every cell in your body. Breathe deeply, and with each breath you take, connect the light that flows down from heaven through your feet into the earth beneath your feet. Feel the connection of heaven and earth that flows in and through you. Hold each breath for a moment, savoring this precious connection. As you exhale, focus on releasing the shadows that haunt your dreams and steal your strength. Continue to breathe in and out until you rest in the arms of Love.

–OR–

Lighting the Advent Candle of Love
(with children)

(If you are worshiping with children, invite them to relight the Advent candles of Peace, Hope, and Joy, before lighting the last purple candle. Note that there are only a few more days until you will light the white candle to celebrate Christ's birth on Christmas Eve. Gaze on the candles quietly before reading the response below; or use the response to begin a conversation on how the children see the candles. With older children, try reflecting the questions back to them, inviting them to provide their own answers.)

Child	Why do we light Advent candles?
Adult	*Advent candles remind us of the light of God coming into the world at Christmas.*
Child	How many candles do we light today?
Adult	*We light four candles because this is the fourth week of Advent.*
Child	Why do we relight the first three candles?
Adult	*We relight the Advent candles of Peace, Hope, and Joy because this is a season of peace, hope, and joy.*
Child	Why do we light the fourth candle?
Adult	*This is the Advent candle of Love. We light it because Jesus is God's gift of love to the world.*
Child	So that's why we light the Advent candles.
Adult	*That's why we light the Advent candles.*

Poetic Reflection

"For Unto Us—LOVE," Lo The Poet
https://youtu.be/CQ_RfQl6M-M

Opening Prayer

Your light is love, Loving God, for you are Love—
    love that hovered over the primordial waters,
        calling forth the glory of creation;
    love that filled an unwed mother with your Spirit,
        bringing forth a child who would be the world's
            light and salvation;
    love that taught my heart to lay aside hate,
        anger, and resentment;
    love that seals my name in the book of life.
Open my heart to the light of this love,
    and help me shine with its glory.
I am ready for your coming, Love Incarnate,
    the coming of Love. Amen.

Psalm of Praise (Psalm 59:16)

I will sing of your strength!
    In the morning I will shout out loud
    about your faithful love
    because you have been my stronghold,
    my shelter when I was distraught.

Song: "Lo, How a Rose E'er Blooming"

Charlotte Church *(choir with lyrics)*
https://youtu.be/GifodHw6Hko

23

Scripture Reading
(1 John 4:7-8, 18-19; John 3:16-17)

Dear friends, let's love each other,
    because love is from God,
    and everyone who loves is born from God
    and knows God.
The person who doesn't love does not know God,
    because God is love.
There is no fear in love, but perfect love drives out fear,
    because fear expects punishment.
The person who is afraid has not been made perfect in love.
We love because God first loved us.
God so loved the world that he gave his only Son,
    so that everyone who believes in him won't perish
    but will have eternal life.
God didn't send his Son into the world
    to judge the world,
    but that the world might be saved through him.

Meditation

The gospel in a word is love. Everyone who loves is born of God, because God is Love. It's that simple and that hard. You can't know God when fear and hatred lie in your heart. The only way to find love is by loving. And the only way to love is to abide in God's love. There is no "kinda" loving God or "sorta" loving your neighbor. With love, it's all or nothing. Christ came into the world to reclaim and remake us in the very image of God's Love. John knew that we hide from God because we fear judgment. But to our surprise, we find love instead. We can't truly love God or others if we are constantly afraid of being judged. Julian of Norwich wrote that God looks on us with mercy, not judgment. In our eyes, we do not stand. In God's eyes, we do not fall. Both are true, but the deeper insight belongs to God. We do not fall because God is Love. Today is a day to stand in God's love and allow love to flow through you in everything you say and in everything you do.

Response to the Word

If you have a dog or cat, place your pet in your lap and offer it your love. Look into its eyes and behold the first Incarnation of the Word—the Incarnation brought forth when God spoke the universe into being. Acknowledge the arrogance of thinking that God's salvation and concern starts and ends with the human race. God so loved *the world* . . . . Thank your pet for embodying the miraculous love of this first Incarnation—an Incarnation that existed long before the Incarnate Word came to earth as a baby in Bethlehem.

–OR–

Response to the Word

(Set up a crèche or nativity set, or find an image of one online. Observe the characters gathered around the baby Jesus and reflect on how each comes into the story differently, how each has a unique experience of Jesus and his arrival.)

- As you look at the Nativity set and think about the story, what newness do you find in the Christmas story?

- In what way is God's love making you new this holiday season?

- How is Christmas an expression of God's love for you? In what way are you an expression of God's love for others?

Song: "Love Came Down at Christmas"

Charles Szabo *(piano with lyrics)*
https://youtu.be/Y_znemn_RV4
Ali Matthews *(vocals)*
https://youtu.be/z1c5rxgZNts

Blessing

Love has come.
Be open to its transforming power.
Be prepared to embrace it with a full heart.
Be ready to receive Love Incarnate,
     the coming of Love.

Sending Activities

(Choose an activity or come up with your own way to share God's love in the week ahead.)

- Create or decorate heart ornaments with pre-purchased craft supplies or with a simple paper heart. (Video instruction here: https://youtu.be/2h6jIqOUYcE). Write a loving message, if you want. Deliver the hearts anonymously to neighbors, friends, family, or local shop and restaurant workers.

- Send loving emails, cards, prayers, or calls to friends and families who are sheltering alone this holiday season. If you have young children in your home, encourage them to call grandparents and friends just to say, "I love you!"

- If you have clean (like new) stuffed animals in storage, deliver them to a shelter, hospital, or donation center to be shared with others. (Many places may only accept new items.)

CHAPTER 5
CHRISTMAS EVE

Gathering Music: "*Il Est Né* (He Is Born)"

Michael Gettel *(choir and orchestra)*

https://youtu.be/ba0dVszm3io

Centering Words

In the beginning was a child—and the child was God's salvation, and God was Salvation.

Gathering Words (Isaiah 9:2, 6)

The people walking in darkness have seen a great light. On those living in a pitch-dark land, light has dawned. A child is born to us, a son is given to us, and authority will be on his shoulders. He will be named Wonderful Counselor, Mighty God, Eternal Father, Prince of Peace.

Lighting the Christ Candle
(with adults)

(If you are worshiping alone or with a group of adults, relight the Advent candles of Peace, Hope, Joy, and Love, then light the white Christ candle and follow these instructions.)

As you gaze upon the flickering candles, reflect on the gift we have received this night—the gift of God's utter vulnerability. Centering your attention on your breath, allow this vulnerability to heal your need to be strong, your desire to be self-sufficient, your impulse to control your own destiny. Breathe deeply, and with each breath you take, allow your inner child to connect with the baby Jesus lying helplessly in a manger. With each breath you take, reach out with love and care to this holy child, and feel the Holy One reach back with gifts to heal your brokenness, with mercies to mend your soul. Hold each breath for a moment, praising God for the gift of reclaimed innocence— the gift only a child can offer. As you exhale, focus on releasing the shields you put up to protect yourself from being hurt. Continue to breathe in and out until you can hold the Christ child in the arms of your love.

–OR–

Lighting the Christ Candle
(with children)

(If you are worshiping with children, invite them to relight the Advent candles of Peace, Hope, Joy, and Love. Then have the youngest child light the white Christ candle. Gaze on the candles quietly before reading the response below; or use the response to begin a conversation on how the children see the candles. With older children, try reflecting the questions back to them, inviting them to provide their own answers.)

Child	Why do we relight the Advent candles tonight?
Adult	*We relight the Advent candles because Christmas is also a season of peace, hope, joy, and love.*
Child	Why do we light the white candle?
Adult	*This is the Christ candle.* *We light it to celebrate the birth of Jesus, who was born on this night.*
Child	Why is it in the center of the Advent candles.
Adult	*The Christ candle is in the center because Christ Jesus is the center of our lives.*
Child	So that's why we light the candles.
Adult	*That's why we light the Advent and Christ candles.*

Opening Prayer

Your gift is salvation, Holy One, for you are Salvation—
    salvation born in a world of darkness
        to light my steps in the ways of peace;
    salvation born in a world of despair
        to open my eyes to the promise of hope;
    salvation born in a world of pain
        to free my tongue to sing your joy;
    salvation born in a world of division and hatred
        to free my heart to rest in the arms of your love.
Incarnate Love, touch my spirit with laughter,
    as I worship you with the shepherds
        and sing songs with the angelic chorus
            proclaiming the glory of your salvation.
Amen.

Song: "Angels We Have Heard on High"

Grace Community Church, Sun Valley, CA *(congregation with lyrics)*
https://youtu.be/ihNfepzL48s

Home Free *(a capella vocals)*
https://youtu.be/teSuDu84kMc

Pentatonix *(upbeat a capella vocals)*
https://youtu.be/VAMzAIH12yc

Scripture Reading (Luke 2:1-7)

In those days Caesar Augustus declared that everyone throughout the empire should be enrolled in the tax lists. This first enrollment occurred when Quirinius governed Syria. Everyone went to their own cities to be enrolled. Since Joseph belonged to David's house and family line, he went up from the city of Nazareth in Galilee to David's city, called Bethlehem, in Judea. He went to be enrolled together with Mary, who was promised to him in marriage and who was pregnant. While they were there, the time came for Mary to have her baby. She gave birth to her firstborn child, a son, wrapped him snugly, and laid him in a manger, because there was no place for them in the guestroom.

Song: "What Child Is This"

Kelly Willard *(piano and vocals with lyrics)*
https://youtu.be/DnFVLDVP_x4

Sarah McLachlan *(vocals)*
https://youtu.be/QXYVvPRf7XU

Anna Hawkins ("Christmas Song," *instrumental and vocals*)
https://youtu.be/KfplGJaJCWs

Scripture Reading (Luke 2:8-14)

Nearby shepherds were living in the fields, guarding their sheep at night. The Lord's angel stood before them, the Lord's glory shone around them, and they were terrified. The angel said, "Don't be afraid! Look! I bring good news to you—wonderful, joyous news for all people. Your savior is born today in David's city. He is Christ the Lord. This is a sign for you: you will find a newborn baby wrapped snugly and lying in a manger." Suddenly a great assembly of the heavenly forces was with the angel praising God. They said, "Glory to God in heaven, and on earth peace among those whom [God] favors."

Song: "Hark! the Herald Angels Sing"

(organ and vocals with lyrics)
https://youtu.be/lCt1s44cfMM

Scripture Reading (Luke 2:15-20)

When the angels returned to heaven, the shepherds said to each other, "Let's go right now to Bethlehem and see what's happened. Let's confirm what the Lord has revealed to us." They went quickly and found Mary and Joseph, and the baby lying in the manger. When they saw this, they reported what they had been told about this child. Everyone who heard it was amazed at what the shepherds told them. Mary committed these things to memory and considered them carefully. The shepherds returned home, glorifying and praising God for all they had heard and seen. Everything happened just as they had been told.

Song: "Angels from the Realms of Glory"

Grace Community Church, Sun Valley, CA *(congregation with lyrics)*
https://youtu.be/lUL8CDz2G1k

Piano Guys with Mormon Tabernacle Choir *(instrumental and choir)*
https://youtu.be/ELjgFKACcdQ

Meditation

Either we believe that the creator of heaven and earth was powerless to find proper lodging for Mary to give birth to God's Son, or we must acknowledge that something earth-shattering is going on here. In the birth of the universe, God is revealed as all powerful; in the birth of Jesus, God is revealed as all vulnerable. Only a love that is both all-powerful and all-vulnerable can save the world. Only a love that spreads its arms naked on the cross can save the world. In Christ, God becomes naked and vulnerable to save humankind. Christmas is a time to treasure this love and open our hearts, naked and vulnerable, before the Christ child.

Response to the Word

(Look at your crèche (Nativity set) or find an image of one online. Observe the characters gathered around the baby Jesus and give thanks for his presence in your life. See him as a newborn child, as a wise rabbi and teacher, as a man of God, even as the Risen Christ. Or gaze at a Christmas tree with gifts beneath the tree and reflect on the gifts of this season.)

- What is most precious to you about Jesus's birth?

- What gift does Jesus bring you this holiday season?

- How is Christmas a gift in and of itself?

- How might you be a Christmas gift for someone else?

Song: "Silent Night"

Hillsong *(vocals with lyrics)*
https://youtu.be/UNpiQwgStNA
Isisip *(vocals with lyrics)*
https://youtu.be/hyY36DJmIcs

Blessing

May your home be a place where God is gloried.
May your lives reflect the joy of God's grace.
May your actions bring hope to everyone you meet.
May your spirit abide in peace.

Sending Activities

(Choose an activity or come up with your own way to share the glory of Christ's birth in the week ahead.)

- Tell the world all you have heard and seen.

- Turn your Christmas tree lights on in a darkened room and re-read Isaiah 9:2. Reflect on (or discuss) where you have seen light shine in the darkness this last month.

- Call or video conference a friend or family member who is alone during the holidays and sing a Christmas carol to them.

- Volunteer to help serve a holiday dinner at your local shelter or soup kitchen.

- If you have an Advent calendar, open the last box or hang the last ornament to celebrate the end of Advent and the beginning of the twelve days of Christmas.

CHAPTER 6
FIRST SUNDAY
AFTER CHRISTMAS

Gathering Music: "Peace Has Come"

Hillsong *(vocals with lyrics)*
https://youtu.be/7BFXCd2pWrM

Centering Words

In the beginning was the Word—and the Word was with God, and the Word was God.

Relighting the Candles
(with adults)

(If you are worshiping alone or with a group of adults, relight the Advent candles of Peace, Hope, Joy, and Love, then relight the white Christ candle and follow these instructions.)

As you gaze upon the flickering candles, think about all the people who can't be with you but who you wish to bring into this worship experience with you. Speak their names aloud and envision them in your mind's eye sitting with you in the glow of the candles. Centering your attention on your breath, allow your heart to fill with care and warmth until it feels time to move into prayer.

–OR–

Relighting the Candles
(with children)

(If you are worshiping with children, invite them to relight the Advent candles of Peace, Hope, Joy, Love, and Christ candles. Gaze on the candles quietly before reading the response below; or use the response to begin a conversation on how the children see the candles. With older children, try reflecting the questions back to them, inviting them to provide their own answers.)

Child   Why do we keep lighting the candles
now that Christmas is over?

*Adult   We relight the Advent and Christ candles
to remind us that Christmas is a season
of peace, hope, joy, and love,
and that Jesus remains the center of our lives.*

Child   How long will we light the candles?

*Adult   We will light the candles through the twelve days
of the Christmas season, which ends next week
when we celebrate the arrival of the three kings.*

Child   So that's why keep lighting the candles.

Adult   That's why we keep lighting the candles.

Opening Prayer

Word of God, Lord of Life, Light of light,
    speak into the void once more,
        that creation may shine with your glory.
Come into my aching heart,
    and heal my troubled spirit,
        that your Life may flow within me this day.
Show me the power of your Light
    to dispel the darkness,
        and claim me as your beloved child.
Shine the light of your love
    into every corner of the earth,
        that all who walk in darkness
            may behold the brightness
                of your dawn. Amen.

Psalm of Praise (Psalm 104:1-2, 4-5)

LORD my God, how fantastic you are!
You are clothed in glory and grandeur!
You wear light like a robe;
    you open the skies like a curtain.
You make the winds your messengers;
    you make fire and flame your ministers.
You established the earth on its foundations
    so that it will never ever fall.

Song: "It Came Upon the Midnight Clear"

Chris Tomlin, "Midnight Clear (Love Song)"
(vocals with lyrics/guitar chords)
https://youtu.be/E4tGVUX3YqI

Scripture Reading (John 1:1-5, 9, 14)

In the beginning was the Word
    and the Word was with God
    and the Word was God.
The Word was with God in the beginning.
Everything came into being through the Word,
    and without the Word
    nothing came into being.
What came into being
    through the Word was life,
    and the life was the light for all people.
The light shines in the darkness,
    and the darkness doesn't extinguish the light.
The true light that shines on all people
    was coming into the world.

The Word became flesh
> and made his home among us.
We have seen his glory,
> glory like that of a father's only son,
> full of grace and truth.

Meditation

Like Genesis 1 and 2, John 1 is a creation story. The Word that came down at Christmas is the same Word that spoke creation into existence. From the beginning, light and life came into the world through the Word, and the darkness was not able to overcome the light. All who live in this Light are children of light, and children of Life itself. But just as the darkness doesn't extinguish the light, neither does the light extinguish the darkness. The light shines *in* the darkness and we face a decision with every choice we make: will we live as children of light or will we not? This is a day to shine the Word's Light within and soberly appraise where shadows continue to lurk.

Response to the Word

(Gaze at the Christ candle you lit a few minutes earlier, or stare at a candle image online, even a sunny or moonlit sky outside.)

- How does light change our experience of an event?

- How does the light of Christ change our experience of even a strange holiday season?

- Where are you needing more light? How might you find that light?

- Where or how might you be light for another?

Song: "This Little Light of Mine"

(choir with lyrics)

https://www.youtube.com/watch?v=dxZmKxGI7j0&vl=en

Bruce Springsteen with the Sessions Band in Dublin *(vocals)*

https://youtu.be/R0qAYq1GVec

Blessing

The Word, who was with God in the beginning,
   is your life and light.
Walk in darkness no longer.
Your light has come.
Hold firm to the life that truly is Life.

Sending Activities

(Choose an activity or come up with your own way to share God's light in the week ahead.)

- Turn your Christmas tree lights on in a darkened room and re-read John 1:4-5. Reflect on (or discuss) how and where you might shine light in the year ahead.

- If people came to mind during the Advent candle reflection, pray for them each day for the remainder of the Christmas season that ends January 6 on Epiphany). Send them a card or email to let them know you are thinking about and praying for them.

- If you have an Advent calendar, review each of the boxes or look at each of the twenty-four ornaments. Reflect on (or discuss) which one meant the most to you this past month.

- During the week, sing or listen to "The Twelve Days of Christmas." Allow the gift of laughter and merriment to enter and bless your Christmas season. While most people agree that the song was written and sung purely for fun, imagine what each day's characters might represent if they were clues to understanding tenants of the Christian faith. To learn more about "the holiday's most annoying carol," and see the lengths people will go to turn it into a theological primer, go to: https://www. vox.com/2015/12/25/10661878/12-days-of-christmas -explained.

- If you didn't do so earlier in the month, place a tea-light on each doorstep in your neighborhood with an index card saying: "Wishing you light and love."

- Support a charity that raises money to harness solar energy for light and electricity in developing nations.

CHAPTER 7
EPIPHANY OF THE LORD

Gathering Music: "Light Our Way"

The Florin Street Band *(vocals)*
https://youtu.be/nxeETbr864M

Centering Words

Arise, shine! Your light has come. Darkness fades like a passing dream. Follow the light of the world.

Relighting the Candles
(with adults)

(If you are worshiping alone or with a group of adults, relight the Advent candles of Peace, Hope, Joy, and Love, then relight the white Christ candle and follow these instructions.)

As you gaze upon the Christ candle, travel back in time to see a star shining in the night sky announcing Christ's birth. Allow the light to take you with the wise men on a journey of discovery—a journey is meant to alter your life forever. Ask the light of Christ to bless you with gifts of knowledge and wisdom, kindness and goodness, patience and humility, goodness and faithfulness, love and joy, gentleness and peace. Claim these gifts with every breath you take, then travel back to the present to offer your own gifts back to God on this Epiphany Sunday.

–OR–

Relighting the Candles
(with children)

(If you are worshiping with children, invite them to relight the Advent candles of Peace, Hope, Joy, Love, and Christ candles. Gaze on the candles quietly before reading the response below; or use the response to begin a conversation on how the children see the candles. With older children, try reflecting the questions back to them, inviting them to provide their own answers.)

Child	Why do we keep lighting the candles?
Adult	*We keep lighting the candles*
	because Christmas is more than just a day.
	It's an entire season of peace, hope, joy, and love.
	A season that ends today.
Child	What's so special about today?
Adult	*Today is called Epiphany.*
	It's the day we celebrate the appearance
	of Wise Men from the East, who followed a star
	to find Jesus when he was a child.
Child	What did they bring him?
Adult	*These three kings brought gifts of gold,*
	frankincense, and myrrh.
Child	So that's why keep lighting the candles.
Adult	*That's why we keep lighting the candles.*

Opening Prayer

God of starlight, disperse the darkness,
    that I may behold the light of your love
        shining in my life.
Lift my eyes to behold your glory,
    and guide me like the kings of old
        in a journey of mystery at Christ's coming—
        a coming announced in the heavens
          in Jesus's natal star. Amen.

Psalm of Praise (Psalm 27:1 NIV)

The LORD is my light and my salvation—
 whom shall I fear?
The LORD is the stronghold of my life—
 of whom shall I be afraid?

Song: "The First Noel"

SE Samonte *(a capella vocals with lyrics)*
https://youtu.be/tvAJqK9a6Bw

Pentatonix *(a capella vocals)*
https://youtu.be/0u5UvnKlCTA

Scripture Reading (Matthew 2:1-12)

After Jesus was born in Bethlehem in the territory of Judea during the rule of King Herod, magi came from the east to Jerusalem. They asked, "Where is the newborn king of the Jews? We've seen his star in the east, and we've come to honor him."

When King Herod heard this, he was troubled, and everyone in Jerusalem was troubled with him. He gathered all the chief priests and the legal experts and asked them where the Christ was to be born. They said, "In Bethlehem of Judea, for this is what the prophet wrote:

"You, Bethlehem, land of Judah,
 by no means are you least among the rulers of Judah,
 because from you will come one who governs,
 who will shepherd my people Israel."

Then Herod secretly called for the magi and found out from them the time when the star had first appeared. He sent them to Bethlehem, saying, "Go and search carefully for the child. When you've found him, report to me so that I too may go and honor him." When they heard the king, they went; and look, the star they had seen in the east went ahead of them until it stood over the place where the child was. When they saw the star, they were filled with joy. They entered the house and saw the child with Mary his mother. Falling to their knees, they honored him. Then they opened their treasure chests

43

and presented him with gifts of gold, frankincense, and myrrh. Because they were warned in a dream not to return to Herod, they went back to their own country by another route.

Meditation

The magi from the east spent their lives studying obscure texts and looking for signs in the heavens. They were learned, hopeful, expectant, but patient kings. When a star arose in the west, they knew it meant the arrival of someone extraordinary—someone who could change the world, someone worthy of their gifts and devotion. Though our crèches and our Christmas nativity plays place the wise men at the stable with the shepherds, their journey took them two years before they reached Herod. Like the early disciples who left their nets and families to follow Jesus, the magi left their kingdoms behind to undertake a journey worth taking. We marvel at the riches they brought the holy family, but we rarely give a passing thought to the journey itself. Our faith is a journey from the cradle to the grave and it is full of signs and wonders—if we look to our sacred texts and learn how to read the signs God places in our lives when the time is right. May we too be learned, hopeful, expectant, and patient.

Response to the Word

(Take a look at a crèche (Nativity set) with the sages gathered around the baby Jesus. Reflect on their gifts, or gaze at a Christmas tree, which may empty or littered with the mess of unwrapped gifts scattered around.)

- How has Christmas been a gift to you this year?

- What gifts have you missed this year?

- How might you find those gifts or let go of your yearning for those gifts?

- How might you be or bring a gift to another?

Song: "We Three Kings"

Jennifer Avalon *(vocals with lyrics)*
https://youtu.be/k8mjRxkMBkE

The Hound + The Fox *(vocals)*
https://youtu.be/eEtUGgBwzEM
(Pause when the video ends at 3:22 to avoid advertisement for the album.)

Blessing

Follow the star of Christ's birth.
Journey with kings of old in search of God's Son.
Walk with the magi in search of meaning and purpose.
Live in God's blessings
    and shine as a light to the nations.

Sending Activities

(Choose an activity or come up with your own way to share the light of Epiphany in the week ahead.)

- Look at the crèche or nativity set you've set up, or find an image of one online. Place the kings at the center of the scene, as they offer their gifts to the child Jesus. Reflect on (or discuss) what gift you would bring to Jesus if you were there.

- Watch or sing "The Little Drummer Boy" to deepen your reflection on the gifts you might bring to honor Christ's birth and presence in our world.

- If you are physically able, offer to take down a neighbor's Christmas lights for them in the week or month ahead.

- For most of Christian history, Epiphany was the day for gift-giving, and still remains so in some cultures. Deliver or send simple Epiphany gifts (packaged chocolates, scented soap, a candle, incense, etc.) to neighbors and friends this week.

(Epiphany actually falls on January 6 each year, so you have a few days to if you're celebrating on Sunday.)

- Call your favorite charity or church and ask what help or donation they most need as the holiday season comes to a close. Or ask if they know of an individual or family who has a particular need. If possible, offer to fulfill or donate toward that need. Keep the individual or family in your prayers for the first month.